The Song of the Stone Wall

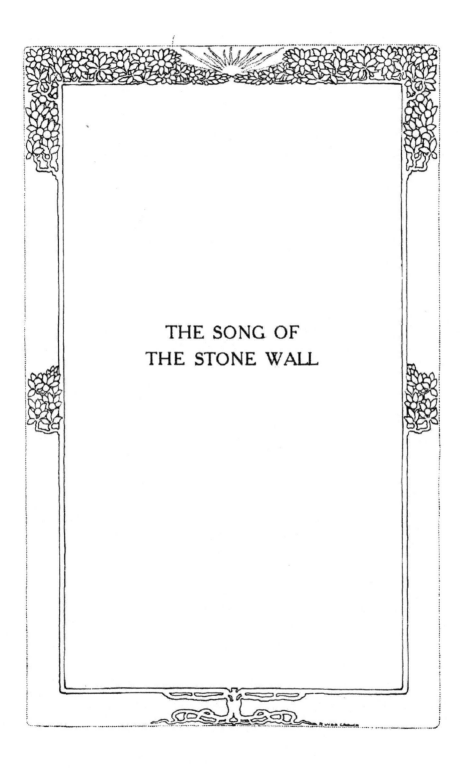

THE SONG OF
THE STONE WALL

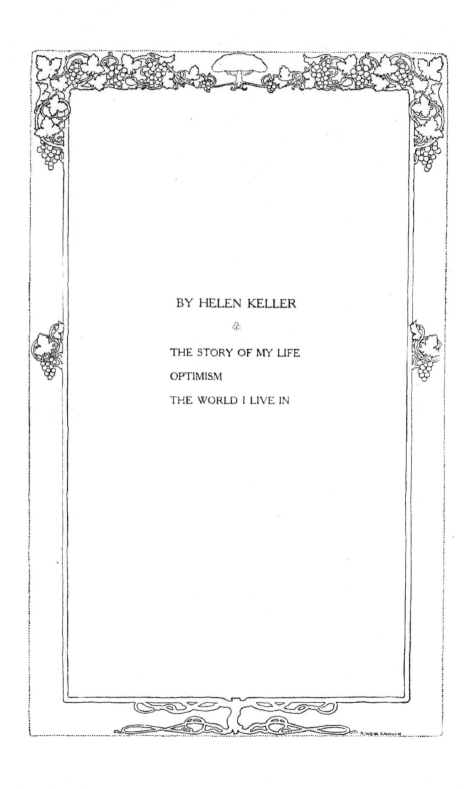

BY HELEN KELLER

THE STORY OF MY LIFE

OPTIMISM

THE WORLD I LIVE IN

THE SONG OF
THE STONE WALL

BY
HELEN KELLER

NEW YORK
THE CENTURY CO.
1910

DEDICATION

WHEN I began "The Song of the Stone Wall," Dr. Edward Everett Hale was still among us, and it was my intention to dedicate the poem to him if it should be deemed worthy of publication. I fancied that he would like it; for he loved the old walls and the traditions that cling about them.

As I tried to image the men who had built the walls long ago, it seemed to me that Dr. Hale was the living embodiment of whatever was heroic in the founders of New England. He was a great American. He was also a great Puritan. Was not the zeal of his ancestors upon his lips, and their courage in his heart? Had they not bequeathed to him their torch-like faith, their patient fervor of toil and their creed of equality?

But his bright spirit had inherited no trace of their harshness and gloom. The windows of his soul opened to the sunlight of a joyous faith. His optimism and genial humor inspired gladness and good sense in others. With an old

story he prepared their minds to receive new ideas, and with a parable he opened their hearts to generous feelings. All men loved him because he loved them. They knew that his heart was in their happiness, and that his humanity embraced their sorrows. In him the weak found a friend, the unprotected, a champion. Though a herald and proclaimer of peace, he could fight stubbornly and passionately on the side of justice. His was a lovable, uplifting greatness which drew all men near and ever nearer to God and to each other. Like his ancestors, he dreamed of a land of freedom founded on the love of God and the brotherhood of man, a land where each man shall achieve his share of happiness and learn the work of manhood—to rule himself and "lend a hand."

Thoughts like these were often in my mind as the poem grew and took form. It is fitting, therefore, that I should dedicate it to him, and in so doing I give expression to the love and reverence which I have felt for him ever since he called me his little cousin, more than twenty years ago.

HELEN KELLER

Wrentham, Massachusetts,
    January, 1910.

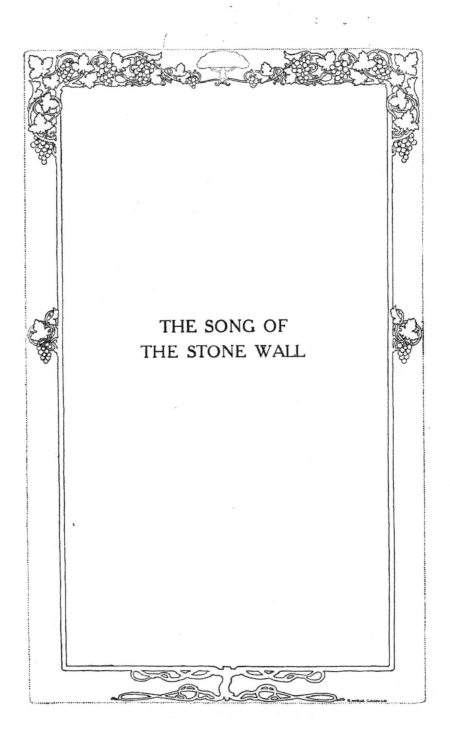
THE SONG OF THE STONE WALL

THE SONG OF
THE STONE WALL

Come walk with me, and I will tell

What I have read in this scroll of stone;

I will spell out this writing on hill and meadow.

It is a chronicle wrought by praying workmen,

The forefathers of our nation—

Leagues upon leagues of sealèd history await-

    ing an interpreter.

This is New England's tapestry of stone

Alive with memories that throb and quiver

At the core of the ages

As the prophecies of old at the heart of God's

Word.

The walls have many things to tell me,

And the days are long. I come and listen:

My hand is upon the stones, and the tale I

fain would hear

Is of the men who built the walls,

And of the God who made the stones and

the workers.

With searching feet I walk beside the wall;

I plunge and stumble over the fallen stones;

I follow the windings of the wall

Over the heaving hill, down by the meadow-

brook,

Beyond the scented fields, by the marsh where

rushes grow.

On I trudge through pine woods fragrant and

cool

And emerge amid clustered pools and by

rolling acres of rye.

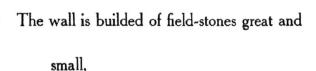

The wall is builded of field-stones great and small,

Tumbled about by frost and storm,

Shaped and polished by ice and rain and sun;

Some flattened, grooved, and chiseled

By the inscrutable sculpture of the weather;

Some with clefts and rough edges harsh to the touch.

Gracious Time has glorified the wall

And covered the historian stones with a mantle of green.

Sunbeams flit and waver in the rifts,

Vanish and reappear, linger and sleep,

Conquer with radiance the obdurate angles,

Filter between the naked rents and wind-

    bleached jags.

I understand the triumph and the truth

Wrought into these walls of rugged stone.

They are a miracle of patient hands,

They are a victory of suffering, a pæan of

    pain;

All pangs of death, all cries of birth,

Are in the mute, moss-covered stones;

They are eloquent to my hands.

O beautiful, blind stones, inarticulate and

dumb!

In the deep gloom of their hearts there is a

gleam

Of the primeval sun which looked upon them

When they were begotten.

So in the heart of man shines forever

A beam from the everlasting sun of God.

Rude and unresponsive are the stones;

Yet in them divine things lie concealed;

I hear their imprisoned chant:—

"We are fragments of the universe,

Chips of the rock whereon God laid the

foundation of the world:

Out of immemorial chaos He wrought us.

Out of the sun, out of the tempest, out of the

travail of the earth we grew.

We are wonderfully mingled of life and death;

We serve as crypts for innumerable, unnoticed,

    tiny forms.

We are manifestations of the Might

That rears the granite hills unto the clouds

And sows the tropic seas with coral isles.

We are shot through and through with hidden

    color;

A thousand hues are blended in our gray

    substance.

Sapphire, turquoise, ruby, opal,

Emerald, diamond, amethyst, are our sisters

    from the beginning,

And our brothers are iron, lead, zinc,

Copper and silver and gold.

We are the dust of continents past and to come,

We are a deathless frieze carved with man's

    destiny;

In us is the record sibylline of far events.

We are as old as the world, our birth was

    before the hills.

We are the cup that holds the sea

And the framework of the peak that parts the

    sky.

When Chaos shall again return,

And endless Night shall spread her wings

upon a ruined world,

We alone shall stand up from the shattered earth,

Indestructible, invincible witnesses of God's

eternal purpose."

In reflective mood by the wall I wander;

The hoary stones have set my heart astir;

My thoughts take shape and move beside me

in the guise

Of the stern men who built the wall in early

olden days.

One by one the melancholy phantoms go

stepping from me,

And I follow them in and out among the stones.

I think of the days long gone,

Flown like birds beyond the ramparts of the

world.

The patient, sturdy men who piled the stones

Have vanished, like the days, beyond the

bounds

Of earth and mortal things.

From their humble, steadfast lives has sprung

    the greatness of my nation.

I am bone of their bone, breath of their

    breath,

Their courage is in my soul.

The wall is an Iliad of granite: it chants to me

Of pilgrims of the perilous deep,

Of fearless journeyings and old forgotten

    things.

The blood of grim ancestors warms the fingers

That trace the letters of their story;

My pulses beat in unison with pulses that are

stilled;

The fire of their zeal inspires me

In my struggle with darkness and pain.

These embossed books, unobliterated by the

tears and laughter of Time,

Are signed with the vital hands of undaunted

men.

I love these monoliths, so crudely imprinted

With their stalwart, cleanly, frugal lives.

From my seat among the stones I stretch

my hand and touch

My friend the elm, urnlike, lithesome, tall.

Far above the reach of my exploring fingers

Birds are singing and winging joyously

Through leafy billows of green.

The elm-tree's song is wondrous sweet;

The words are the ancientest language of trees —

They tell how earth and air and light

Are wrought anew to beauty and to fruitfulness.

I feel the glad stirrings under her rough bark;

Her living sap mounts up to bring forth leaves;

Her great limbs thrill beneath the wand of

spring.

This wall was builded in our fathers'

days —

Valorous days when life was lusty and the

land was new.

Resemble the walls the builders, buffeted,

stern, and worn.

To us they left the law,

Order, simplicity, obedience,

And the wall is the bond they gave the nation

At its birth of courage and unflinching faith.

Before the epic here inscribed began,

They wrote their course upon a trackless sea.

O, tiny craft, bearing a nation's seed!

Frail shallop, quick with unborn states!

Autumn was mellow in the fatherland when

    they set sail,

And winter deepened as they neared the West.

Out of the desert sea they came at last,

And their hearts warmed to see that frozen land.

O, first gray dawn that filtered through the dark!

Bleak, glorious birth-hour of our northern states!

They stood upon the shore like new created men;

On barren solitudes of sand they stood,

The conquered sea behind, the unconquered wilderness before.

Some died that year beneath the cruel cold,

And some for heartsick longing and the pang

Of homes remembered and souls torn asunder.

That spring the new-plowed field for bread of

life

Bordered the new-dug acre marked for death;

Beside the springing corn they laid in the

sweet, dark earth

The young man, strong and free, the maiden,

fair and trustful,

The little child, and the uncomplaining mother.

Across the meadow, by the ancient pines,

Where I, the child of life that lived that spring,

Drink in the fragrances of the young year,

The field-wall meets one grimly squared and

straight.

Beyond it rise the old tombs, gray and restful,

And the upright slates record the generations.

Stiffly aslant before the northern blasts,

Like the steadfast, angular beliefs

Of those whom they commemorate, the head-

stones stand,

Cemented deep with moss and invisible roots.

The rude inscriptions charged with faith and love,

Graceless as Death himself, yet sweet as Death,

Are half erased by the impartial storms.

As children lisping words which move to laughter

Are themselves poems of unconscious melody,

So the old gravestones with their crabbed muse

Are beautiful for their halting words of faith,

Their groping love that had no gift of song.

But all the broken tragedy of life

And all the yearning mystery of death

Are celebrated in sweet epitaphs of vines and

violets.

Close by the wall a peristyle of pines

Sings requiems to all the dead that sleep.

Beyond the village churchyard, still and

calm,

Steeped in the sweetness of eternal morn,

The wall runs down in crumbling cadence

Beside the brook which plays

Through the land like a silver harp.

A wind of ancient romance blows across the

field,

A sweet disturbance thrills the air;

The silken skirts of Spring go rustling by,

And the earth is astir with joy.

Up the hill, romping and shaking their golden

heads,

Come the little children of the wood.

From ecstasy to ecstasy the year mounts

upward.

Up from the south come the odor-laden

winds,

Angels and ministers of life,

Dropping seeds of fruitfulness

Into the bosoms of flowers.

Elusive, alluring secrets hide in wood and

hedge

Like the first thoughts of love

In the breast of a maiden;

The witchery of love is in rock and tree.

Across the pasture, star-sown with daisies,

I see a young girl—the spirit of spring she

    seems,

Sister of the winds that run through the

    rippling daisies.

Sweet and clear her voice calls father and

    brother,

And one whose name her shy lips will not

    utter.

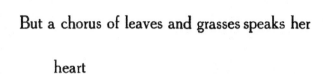

But a chorus of leaves and grasses speaks her heart

And tells his name: the birches flutter by the wall;

The wild cherry-tree shakes its plumy head

And whispers his name; the maple

Opens its rosy lips and murmurs his name;

The marsh-marigold sends the rumor

Down the winding stream, and the blue flag

Spreads the gossip to the lilies in the lake:

All Nature's eyes and tongues conspire

In the unfolding of the tale

That Adam and Eve beneath the blossoming

rose-tree

Told each other in the Garden of Eden.

Once more the wind blows from the walls,

And I behold a fair young mother;

She stands at the lilac-shaded door

With her baby at her breast;

She looks across the twilit fields and smiles

And whispers to her child: "Thy father

comes!"

Life triumphed over many-weaponed Death.

Sorrow and toil and the wilderness thwarted

their stout invasion;

But with the ship that sailed again went no

retreating soul!

Stubborn, unvanquished, clinging to the skirts

of Hope,

They kept their narrow foothold on the land,

And the ship sailed home for more.

With yearlong striving they fought their way

into the forest;

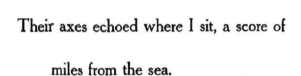

Their axes echoed where I sit, a score of

miles from the sea.

Slowly, slowly the wilderness yielded

To smiling grass-plots and clearings of yellow

corn;

And while the logs of their cabins were still

moist

With odorous sap, they set upon the hill

The shrine of liberty for man's mind,

And by it the shrine of liberty for man's soul,

The school-house and the church.

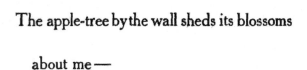

The apple-tree by the wall sheds its blossoms

   about me —

A shower of petals of light upon darkness.

From Nature's brimming cup I drink a

   thousand scents;

At noon the wizard sun stirs the hot soil

   under the pines.

I take the top stone of the wall in my hands

And the sun in my heart;

I feel the rippling land extend to right and

   left,

Bearing up a receptive surface to my uncertain

feet;

I clamber up the hill and beyond the grassy

sweep;

I encounter a chaos of tumbled rocks.

Piles of shadow they seem, huddling close to

the land.

Here they are scattered like sheep,

Or like great birds at rest,

There a huge block juts from the giant wave

of the hill.

At the foot of the aged pines the maiden's

moccasins

Track the sod like the noiseless sandals of

Spring.

Out of chinks in the wall delicate grasses wave,

As beauty grew out of the crannies of those

hard souls.

Joyously, gratefully, after their long wrestling

With the bitter cold and the harsh white

winter,

They heard the step of Spring on the edge of

melting snow-drifts;

Gladly, with courage that flashed from their

life-beaten souls,

As the fire-sparks fly from the hammered stone,

They hailed the fragrant arbutus;

Its sweetness trailed beside the path that they

cut through the forest,

And they gave it the name of their ship

Mayflower.

Beauty was at their feet, and their eyes

beheld it;

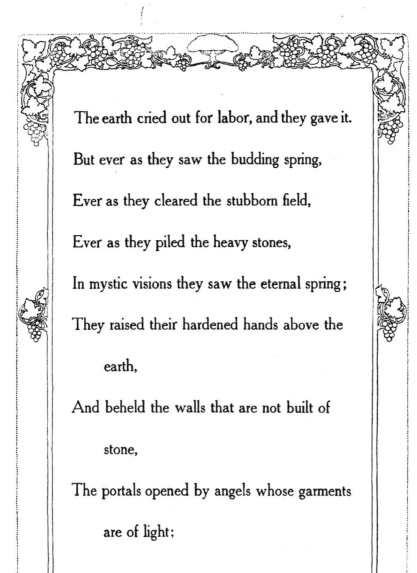

The earth cried out for labor, and they gave it.

But ever as they saw the budding spring,

Ever as they cleared the stubborn field,

Ever as they piled the heavy stones,

In mystic visions they saw the eternal spring;

They raised their hardened hands above the earth,

And beheld the walls that are not built of stone,

The portals opened by angels whose garments are of light;

And beyond the radiant walls of living stones

They dreamed vast meadows and hills of

fadeless green.

In the old house across the road

With weather-beaten front, like the furrowed

face of an old man,

The lights are out forever, the windows are

broken,

And the oaken posts are warped;

The storms beat into the rooms as the passion

of the world

Racked and buffeted those who once dwelt

in them.

The psalm and the morning prayer are silent.

But the walls remain visible witnesses of faith

That knew no wavering or shadow of turning.

They have withstood sun and northern blast,

They have outlasted the unceasing strife

Of forces leagued to tear them down.

Under the stars and the clouds, under the

summer sun,

Beaten by rain and wind, covered with

tender vines,

The walls stand symbols of a granite race,

The measure and translation of olden times.

  In the rough epic of their life, their toil,

    their creeds,

Their psalms, their prayers, what stirring tales

Of days that were their past had they to tell

Their children to keep the new faith burning?

Tales of grandsires in the fatherland

Whose faith was seven times tried in fiery

    furnaces,—

Of Rowland Taylor who kissed the stake,

And stood with hands folded and eyes stead-
fastly turned

To the sky, and smiled upon the flames;

Of Latimer, and of Cranmer who for
cowardice heroically atoned —

Who thrust his right hand into the fire

Because it had broken plight with his heart

And written against the voice of his
conviction.

With such memories they exalted and
cherished

The heroism of their tried souls,

And ours are wrung with doubt and self-

distrust!

I am kneeling on the odorous earth;

The sweet, shy feet of Spring come tripping

o'er the land,

Winter is fled to the hills, leaving snowy

wreaths

On apple-tree, meadow, and marsh.

The walls are astir; little waves of blue

Run through my fingers murmuring:

" We follow the winds and the snow ! "

Their heart is a cup of gold.

Soft whispers of showers and flowers

Are mingled in the spring song of the walls.

Hark to the songs that go singing like the wind

Through the chinks of the wall and thrill the

heart

And quicken it with passionate response !

The walls sing the song of wild bird, the

hoof-beat of deer,

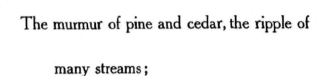

The murmur of pine and cedar, the ripple of

many streams;

Crows are calling from the Druidical wood;

The morning mist still haunts the meadows

Like the ghosts of the wall builders.

As I listen, methinks I hear the bitter plaint

Of the passing of a haughty race,

The wronged, friendly, childlike, peaceable

tribes,

The swarthy archers of the wilderness,

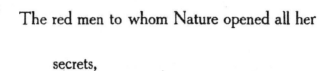

The red men to whom Nature opened all her

secrets,

Who knew the haunts of bird and fish,

The hidden virtue of herb and root;

All the travail of man and beast they knew—

Birth and death, heat and cold,

Hunger and thirst, love and hate;

For these are the unchanging things writ in the

imperishable book of life

That man suckled at the breast of woman

must know.

In the dim sanctuary of the pines

The winds murmur their mysteries through

dusky aisles —

Secrets of earth's renewal and the endless

cycle of life.

Living things are afoot among the grasses;

The closed fingers of the ferns unfold,

New bees explore new flowers, and the brook

Pours virgin waters from the rushing founts of

May.

In the old walls there are sinister voices—

The groans of women charged with witchcraft.

I see a lone, gray, haggard woman standing

at bay,

Helpless against her grim, sin-darkened judges.

Terror blanches her lips and makes her

confess

Bonds with demons that her heart knows not.

Satan sits by the judgment-seat and laughs.

The gray walls, broken, weatherworn oracles,

Sing that she was once a girl of love and

laughter,

Then a fair mother with lullabies on her lips,

Caresses in her eyes, who spent her days

In weaving warmth to keep her brood against

the winter cold.

And in her tongue was the law of kindness;

For her God was the Lord Jehovah.

Enemies uprose and swore her accursed,

Laid at her door the writhing forms of

little children,

And she could but answer: "The Evil One

Torments them in my shape."

She stood amazed before the tribunal of her

church

And heard the gates of God's house closed

against her.

Oh, shuddering the silence of the throng,

And fearful the words spoken from the

judgment-seat!

She raised her white head and clasped her

wrinkled hands:

"Pity me, Lord, pity my anguish!

Nor, since Thou art a just and terrible God,

Forget to visit thy wrath upon these people;

For they have sworn away the life of Thy

servant

Who hath lived long in the land keeping Thy

commandments.

I am old, Lord, and betrayed;

By neighbor and kin am I betrayed;

A Judas kiss hath marked me for a witch.

Possessed of a devil? Here be a legion of devils!

Smite them, O God, yea, utterly destroy them

that persecute the innocent."

Before this mother in Israel the judges

cowered ;

But still they suffered her to die.

Through the tragic, guilty walls I hear the

sighs

Of desolate women and penitent, remorseful

men.

Sing of happier themes, O many-voiced epic,

Sing how the ages, like thrifty husbandmen,

winnow the creeds of men,

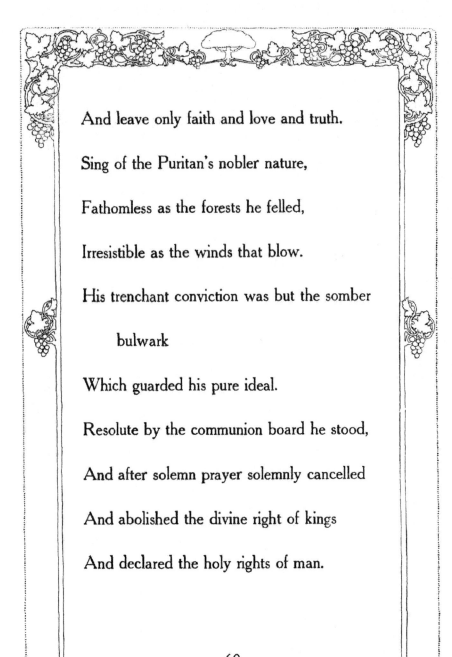

And leave only faith and love and truth.

Sing of the Puritan's nobler nature,

Fathomless as the forests he felled,

Irresistible as the winds that blow.

His trenchant conviction was but the somber

    bulwark

Which guarded his pure ideal.

Resolute by the communion board he stood,

And after solemn prayer solemnly cancelled

And abolished the divine right of kings

And declared the holy rights of man.

Prophet and toiler, yearning for other worlds,

yet wise in this;

Scornful of earthly empire and brooding on

death,

Yet wresting life out of the wilderness

And laying stone on stone the foundation of a

temporal state!

I see him standing at his cabin-door at eventide

With dreaming, fearless eyes gazing at sunset

hills;

In his prophetic sight Liberty, like a bride,

Hasteth to meet her lord, the westward-going

man!

Even as he saw the citadel of Heaven,

He beheld an earthly state divinely fair and just.

Mystic and statesman, maker of homes,

Strengthened by the primal law of toil,

And schooled by monarch-made injustices,

He carried the covenant of liberty with fire

and sword,

And laid a rich state on frugality!

Many republics have sprung into being,

Full-grown, equipped with theories forged in

reason;

All, all have fallen in a single night;

But to the wise, fire-hardened Puritan

Democracy was not a blaze of glory

To crackle for an hour and be quenched out

By the first gust that blows across the world.

I see him standing at his cabin-door,

And all his dreams are true as when he

dreamed them;

But only shall they be fulfilled if we

Are mindful of the toil that gave him power,

Are brave to dare a wilderness of wrong;

So long shall Nature nourish us and Spring

Throw riches in the lap of man

As we beget no wasteful, weak-handed

    generations,

But bend us to the fruitful earth in toil.

Beyond the wall a new-plowed field lies

    steaming in the sun,

And down the road a merry group of children

Run toward the village school.

Hear, O hear! In the historian walls

Rises the beat and tumult of the struggle for

freedom.

Sacred, blood-stained walls, your peaceful

front

Sheltered the fateful fires of Lexington;

Builded to fence green fields and keep the

herds at pasture,

Ye became the frowning breastworks of stern

battle;

Lowly boundaries of the freeman's farm,

Ye grew the rampart of a land at war;

And still ye cross the centuries

Between the age of monarchs and the age

When farmers in their fields are kings.

From the Revolution the young Republic

emerged,

She mounted up as on the wings of the eagle,

She ran and was not weary, and all the

children of the world

Joined her and followed her shining path.

But ever as she ran, above her lifted head

Darkened the monster cloud of slavery.

Hark! In the walls, amid voices of prayer

and of triumph,

I hear the clank of manacles and the ominous

mutterings of bondmen!

At Gettysburg, our Golgotha, the sons of the

fathers

Poured their blood to wash out a nation's

shame.

Cleansed by tribulation and atonement,

The broken nation rose from her knees,

And with hope reborn in her heart set forth

    again

Upon the open road to ideal democracy.

    Sing, walls, in lightning words that shall

    cause the world to vibrate,

Of the democracy to come,

Of the swift, teeming, confident thing!

We are part of it — the wonder and the

    terror and the glory!

Fearless we rush forward to meet the years,

The years that come flying toward us

With wings outspread, agleam on the horizon

of time!

O eloquent, sane walls, instinct with a

new faith,

Ye are barbarous, incongruous, but great with

the greatness of reality.

Walls wrought in unfaltering effort,

Sing of our prosperity, the joyous harvest

Of the labor of lusty toilers.

Down through the years comes the ring of

their victorious axes:

"Ye are titans of the forest, but we are

stronger;

Ye are strong with the strength of mighty

winds,

But we are strong with the unconquerable

strength of souls!"

Still the young race, unassailable, inviolate,

Shakes the solitudes with the strokes of

creation;

Doubly strong we renew the valorous days,

And like a measureless sea we overflow

The fresh green, benevolent West,

The buoyant, fruitful West that dares and sings!

Pure, dew-dripping walls that guard

The quiet, lovable, fertile fields,

Sing praises to Him who from the mossy

rocks

Can bid the fountains leap in thirsty lands.

I walk beside the stones through the young

grain,

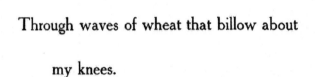

Through waves of wheat that billow about

    my knees.

The wall contests the onward march of the

    wheat;

But the wheat is charged with the life of the

    world;

Its force is irresistible; onward it sweeps,

An engulfing tide, over all the land,

Till hill and valley, field and plain

Are flooded with its green felicity!

Out of the moist earth it has sprung;

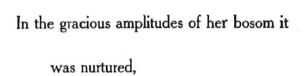

In the gracious amplitudes of her bosom it

    was nurtured,

And in it is wrought the miracle of life.

    Sing, prophetic, mystic walls, of the dreams

        of the builders;

Sing in thundering tones that shall thrill us

To try our dull discontent, our barren wisdom

Against their propagating, unquenchable,

    questionless visions.

Sing in renerving refrain of the resolute men,

Each a Lincoln in his smoldering patience,

Each a Luther in his fearless faith,

Who made a breach in the wall of darkness

And let the hosts of liberty march through.

Calm, eternal walls, tranquil, mature,

Which old voices, old songs, old kisses cover,

As mosses and lichens cover your ancient

stones,

Teach me the secret of your serene repose;

Tell of the greater things to be,

When love and wisdom are the only creed,

And law and right are one.

Sing that the Lord cometh, the Lord cometh,

The fountain-head and spring of life!

Sing, steady, exultant walls, in strains hallowed

and touched with fire,

Sing that the Lord shall build us all together,

As living stones build us, cemented together.

May He who knoweth every pleasant thing

That our sires forewent to teach the peoples

law and truth,

Who counted every stone blessed by their

consecrated hands,

Grant that we remain liberty-loving, sub-

stantial, elemental,

And that faith, the rock not fashioned of

human hands,

Be the stability of our triumphant, toiling days.

CPSIA information can be obtained
at www.ICGtesting.com
Printed in the USA
LVOW04s0738311216
519357LV00003B/126/P